R.M. FOREST

LOVE YOURSELF

The Ultimate Self-Love Handbook, Learn How You Can Love Yourself by Boosting Your Self-Esteem and Healing Your Mind, Body and Soul

Descrierea CIP a Bibliotecii Naţionale a României
R.M. FOREST
LOVE YOURSELF. The Ultimate Self-Love Handbook, Learn How You Can Love Yourself by Boosting Your Self-Esteem and Healing Your Mind, Body and Soul / R.M. Forest – Bucharest: Editura My Ebook, 2021
ISBN

R.M. FOREST

LOVE YOURSELF

The Ultimate Self-Love Handbook, Learn How You Can Love Yourself by Boosting Your Self-Esteem and Healing Your Mind, Body and Soul

My Ebook Publishing House
Bucharest, 2021

TABLE OF CONTENTS

INTRODUCTION

Self-love is perhaps one of the most fundamental yet misunderstood concepts in the world right now. Some dismiss it as a new age ideology that cannot be applied in practical terms. But nothing could be further from the truth. This eBook will show you practical steps with regard to developing self-love. It will also explain what it is and outline the history of the trait and how it has been a core foundation of all spiritual teachings.

Self-love is the ultimate way to boost your self-esteem and become a fully healed and integrated human being. People often come at the idea backwards. They look at attributes such as the way that a confident person walks or observe their traits. But fundamentally, all radical change begins from within. You then start to really value yourself as a powerful creator of your own reality and deserving of love and respect from everybody. Self-love is the opposite of selfish. You cannot love another person unconditionally unless you love yourself first.

Self-love is not about engaging in destructive patterns of behavior and turning a blind eye. It has nothing to do with arrogance or narcissism and everything to do with becoming a fully whole and integrated individual.

When you are able to exercise self-love, your life will become so much easier. This is because you will not sabotage yourself as much, which is what everybody does with their beliefs about unworthiness. You will also have much more stability in your life as you will no longer depend on others for fulfillment. Your emotions and reactions will not be volatile and you will actually become detached (but not uncaring) from a lot of stuff that goes on in the world.

Love is the ultimate building block of the entire universe. Humans are born into the arms of loving parents and die with their loved ones around them (ideally). They live and die by love alone. In the words of Gautama Buddha:

"In the end, only three things matter: how much you loved, how gently you lived, and how gracefully you let go of things not meant for you"

Your ability to love yourself and others is all that really matters. How to get there is another matter entirely. For this, you have to find out who you are and love yourself unconditionally.

Chapter 1

Finding the Self

Finding the self is a mystical concept that has been around since ancient times. The 'self' has been described by many names, such as the soul, the oversoul, the atman, the monad, the "I AM" presence, the Christos, the illumined one, and so on. Labels aside, it can be described as who you truly are without any of the social behaviors and attitudes that you have downloaded since birth. It can be 'found' by shedding illusion and peeling away the layers of programming, which can also be called the ego.

The entire process of childhood and socialization is essentially learning how to forget who we really are. Our peers and parents scold us when we do something that does not conform to their viewpoint. As such, we learn how to behave in such a way that we can be accepted. Being part of a group, family or tribe is the single most important social norm. This dates back to a time where non-conformity would have gotten us thrown out of the tribe - likely to starve or freeze to death. Pleasing others is ingrained deep within us, but it is also very harmful in terms of spiritual evolution.

So when born, we experience traumas in forgetting who we are. And we then have to go through the process of forgetting everything we learned in school and through wider society to find our true selves. Sadly, reconnecting is anything but easy in the modern age. Technology ensures that information is everywhere so we will look everywhere but inside - where the self resides.

How to Find The "Self"

There is a defined path to find the self "quickly", though the process could still hardly be described as quick. Many people are swift to dismiss Eastern modalities as outdated, unusual, and unworkable. But the fact of the matter is that in terms of finding the self, Vedic philosophy occupies a distinct position of respect. To proceed with finding Self, you will need:

1. A silent and serene location
2. The ability to meditate on the heart chakra
3. The ability to severely restrict diet
4. The ability to leave behind all technology and distractions.

In many ways, it is simple and straightforward. Get to a silent location and meditate on loving the self. Restrict your diet so you are not eating any meat, processed food, caffeine, or alcohol.

Avoid technology and eliminate all mental, physical, and emotional distractions.

Though this can be difficult to do, the results will be immense. It is the ideal healing modality. 3 - 7 days is enough for significant changes to occur with the above protocol. It can be repeated as often as necessary and while you won't succeed the first or even the tenth time, it is enough to fully rejuvenate you from the stresses of modern living in a big way.

Ironically, the quickest way to find the self is to do absolutely nothing at all. Your body, mind, and soul will heal if you just stop eating, thinking, and reading garbage material all the time. You will be in a perfect state of health if you stop doing things that put you in a depressed mood and environment. The grand irony of it all is that people feel to need to 'do something' to fix an illusory problem. This leads to fad diets, liposuction, gender changes, unhappy relationships, and unaffordable mortgages.

Vedic philosophy has by no means a stranglehold on silent retreats and fasting. But it really cuts to the heart of the matter with its emphasis on these things and its constant focus on finding the self. There are hundreds of other esoteric modalities such as crystal bowls, visualization, spinning, manifestation, lucid dreaming, chakra work and many more. While they might bring many benefits and even some paranormal effects, they do not cut to the core of finding the self. This involves letting go of everything you have learned to step into new dimensions.

The pinnacle of self-esteem ultimately culminates in self-realization, a state of being that is talked about in practically every piece of spiritual literature of note. This state goes beyond the typical human experience to full bodied bliss and understanding.

However, self-realized people are still flesh and blood, live to tell their experiences, have written books, and can be found by those who actively search for them.

Other Methods to Help Find the Self

There are more ways to try and find who you really are. It is best likened to the peeling of an onion where only the true self is left. A good place to start is to review all of what has happened to you in this lifetime and the major events. The point is not to wallow in them or take pride in achievements. Just draw a linear map of the major events that happened, what their effect on you was, and try to see the bigger picture. This will help to build a degree of objectivity.

In terms of finding self, you do not want to be dependent in any way. So look at all the ways you are emotionally, mentally, physically, or financially dependent on other people and things. Become as self-sufficient as possible. This could entail an eliminating of cigarettes or bad food and finding a new job where you work for yourself. It will be different for everybody.

Finding self is an individual process. Nobody has ever self-realized themselves together. It is just not the way that the universe works. Groupthink is the antithesis of individual empowerment. Because even in groups, solutions only come from one individual with one spark of inspiration. There is no way to share creativity or ingenuity because it comes from within. This means that when you are finding the self, the practices that you use and the philosophy that you adopt will be yours alone. If you simply copy what others are doing, then you are already disempowered, and will never find the self. Without making decisions of your own volition, you are not giving yourself any power.

Chapter 2

Self-Love and the Shadow

Self-Love is a lifelong practice that has to be fully attended to in order to bring about its full effects. In the current era, the law of attraction is very popular and comes with a myriad of benefits. It refers to the fundamental nature of the universe; that we have but one thing in our power, which is our attention. And whatever we turn our attention to, we attract towards us.

Some authors have indicated that attention is love and that whatever we love or put our attention on simply grows bigger. So we must be discerning in where we place our attention. It is worth noting that the two biggest fields in spiritual psychology - shadow work and positivity psychology - are adamant that people should only focus on bettering themselves and will, therefore, better the world as a consequence.

Shadow work is a critical piece of the puzzle in terms or self-realization and empowerment. It has taken centre stage from the law of attraction. According to Carl Jung, enlightenment can only happen through shadow work:

"One does not become enlightened by imagining figures of light, but by making the darkness conscious"

But it is also worth mentioning that when the law of attraction is studied in detail over the course of all the videos and texts, the shadow self is comprehensively dealt with. Over time, the person will attract instances where the dark side becomes healed without making it the main priority. This could be in the dream state or in physical reality.

All About the Shadow

Shadow work has first brought to the mainstream attention through the work of the eminent psychologist and behavioural therapist Carl Jung. he examined the shadow side of the human being primarily through the dream states as well as symbols. He also discovered something called the collective unconscious which is shared by all humans. However, this is not relevant to the personal purpose of finding the self. You do not need to investigate the theory to complete the tasks. The theory always comes second to practical experience.

As per Jung, everybody has a shadow self which needs to be integrated. The less that the person integrates the shadow and expresses it openly, the blacker and denser it will be. Additionally, the shadow will often project its own failings onto other people.

This phenomenon is often demonstrated in law of attraction teachings, where we notice things in others that we hate about ourselves. In other words, our weaknesses and irritation can be the best tools for introspection.

According to some authors, the shadow self is actually the seat of creativity and has many positive aspects. It is just that certain attributes are now viewed upon favourably by our current society. Alternatively, the individual might have just had a certain experience that forced him or her to repress certain emotions and behaviours. Regardless, everybody has a shadow side that needs to be tended to. For some, it is more obvious than others. You can use other people as a mirror to understand your own shadow. It will be oblivious to you but crystal clear to those who know you. For Carl Jung, the shadow self was a monster both individually and collectively:

"It is a frightening thought that man also has a shadow side to him, consisting not just of little weaknesses- and foibles, but of a positively demonic dynamism. The individual seldom knows anything of this; to him, as an individual, it is incredible that he should ever in any circumstances go beyond himself. But let these harmless creatures form a mass, and there emerges a raging monster."

The Dark Side of Self Love

The fact is that human beings learn far more from their pain than they do from their triumphs. We have far more to learn from our faults than our strengths. Mirroring is an excellent technique that everybody would benefit from and can greatly assist in self-love. Everybody can be used as a mirror for our own development.

When we detest somebody else, it is a flaw in our own perception.

What you see in others is a reflection of what you have within yourself but do not want to deal with. As a result, when somebody bothers you, it is easier to project your own failings onto them and criticise. As per German author Hermann Hesse:

"If you hate a person, you hate something in him that is part of yourself. What isn't part of ourselves doesn't disturb us"

Again, this is reflected in the law of attraction. When we judge or condemn others, we are criticizing things we are unable to deal with ourselves. The Christian bible also reflects these teachings:

"You, therefore, have no excuse, you who pass judgement on someone else, for at whatever point you judge another, you are condemning yourself, because you who pass judgement do the same things" (Romans 2:1)

"Do not judge, or you too shall be judged" (Matthew 7:1)

Chapter 3

Building Self-Love

If you want to build up self-love, the first thing that you have to do is purification. The reality is that most people have picked up a lot of wild and irrational beliefs, values and attitudes that are not real. They cause a lot of damage. There are also a lot of physical toxins in the body from an unclean environment.

Purification

You need to purify across all levels in order to love yourself fully. Purification might sound like a drastic step, but it is certainly worth it so you can see yourself with more clarity. Purification generally involves:

1. Fasting or dietary restriction.
2. Information restriction.
3. A natural environment.

4. Meditation.
5. Prayer.
6. Yoga and/or exercise.
7. Reading of uplifting material.
8. Silence.

You can do a combination of the above for as long as you want. 3 days in the minimum and 3 weeks will have incredible benefits.

But any amount is worth doing. These techniques are ancient and despite all of the new age positivity strategies, they work the best.

Nothing will have the same impact as doing the above in tandem with one another. They work individually, but the effects are magnified when combined. It is only when you get away from society (i.e "real" life) and do these practices that you can clearly see just how dysfunctional society really is and how dysfunctional your own beliefs and thoughts are about yourself and about society.

Day to Day Exercises

Not everybody has time for an intense purification exercise. And they can only really be done once every 3 months or so. Due to this, people need less intense modalities so they can build self- love steadily and consistently over time.

The first step is in relation to freeing up your time and energy. Most people have heavy stress from either energy vampires or from work and relationships. The best scenario, if at all possible, is to simply exit a toxic relationship or environment.

Many people are afraid of leaving a job they hate and pretend that they have to stay there to pay the fills. But nothing is worth having your energy drained and living like a zombie with no purpose or intention. What happens is that you are pretending to be someone you are not, which is the polar opposite of authenticity. There are many self-love exercises you can do, but here are 5 of the most effective:

1. The waking and sleeping hours are a prime time to master your thoughts and emotions. In the place between sleeping and waking, turn your thoughts as positive as possible.

These states are more powerful and set the tone for the rest of the day or night.

2. Keeping a gratitude journal is perfect for appreciating what you are and all that you have accomplished. The fact of the matter is that human appreciation is arbitrary and irrational. We can work towards a goal for 5 years and appreciate its completion for a week. We need to reframe our gratitude and appreciation so we can be joyful for everything, not just the big goals.

3. Put yourself first with vacations, massages, extreme sports, concerts, whatever it is that you want to do. You deserve supreme enjoyment, and it is what you are here for. Sadly, most people think that life is supposed to be a painful chore and create stress for themselves. Do not do this to yourself.

4. Stop interfering with others at all costs. There is a kind of virus going around where people are trying to make the world a better place and love pointing out the flaws in the world. This is in spite of the fact that times have never been better, by a gigantic margin. If you do not focus on your own self-

development, you will never develop. And you will find others interfering in your life in a similar fashion.

5. Meditating on love or focusing on the heart chakra is a chief recommendation among ancient spiritual scriptures. The heart chakra is a doorway to the higher self/oversoul if you put your energy there for extended time periods.

Feel Good at All Times

One of the most important and overlooked parts of being able to find the self is being unashamed about feeling good. This entails doing activities that feel good to you as much as possible.

There is a tendency to believe that you must suffer much to 'achieve' happiness. It is more the case that unhappiness has to be 'unlearned' from past conditioning.

There is nothing wrong with feeling good, and nobody is not worthy of self-love, respect, and appreciation. There is actually no reason you have to work for 4 years in university to start out at the corporate ladder and work your way up. This is actually quite silly, given that you can get certified from a distance and set up an online business for a fraction of both the cost and time. Yet people still flock to universities paying tens of thousands of dollars to wait 4 years until they can make an income if they get a job.

In any case, you don't have to accept any limitation that society places upon you. If you want to master self-love, then you have to love yourself and treat yourself with respect. This entails saying no to toxic relationships, setting boundaries, thinking positive thoughts, journaling, getting exercise, taking massages, going for luxurious hot showers, taking regular vacation etc. Your only responsibility is to yourself and to make sure you are as happy as you can be.

Chapter 4

Alternative Self-Love Strategies

There are actually a wide variety of self-love strategies. What's important to understand is that it is not really an additive process. You need to shed the shin or beliefs, values and attitudes that you adopted to protect yourself in this life. Being in a relaxed state of mind helps you to do this. Anything that gives you another perspective and leads you away from erroneous beliefs can be termed a self-love strategy.

Books on Self-Love

Of course, there is no shortage of spiritual teachers who can share a lot of wisdom when it comes to self-love. Krishnamurti, Osho, Alan Watts, Sadhguru, Tolle, the Dalai Lama, the list goes on. All of them offer a different perspective with regard to how to achieve self-realization. But only a select few identify love as the true source and deal with it directly.

One of the modern teachers that does is known as Don Miguel Ruiz, who is a Shaman and proponent of Toltec wisdom. All of his books have been international bestsellers and include The Four Agreements, the Fifth Agreement, The Voice of Knowledge, and The Mastery of Love. Another powerful speaker on self-love is Marianne Williamson. Her first book, A Return to Love had a major impact.

There are many books to choose from in terms of reading. It is important not to be critical or judgemental of any book you read. If it's not for you, just put it down and select another that is more appropriate.

Don’t feel the need to write a 1000 word review about how bad it was. The negativity will just bounce back to you. In any case, love is to be expressed and developed, and there is only so much that you can learn from books alone, regardless of how good the material happens to be. Practice beats theory.

Quickest Paths to Self-Love

To love yourself, you must look at yourself clearly. And doing this is not as easy as you might think. Most people have an idea of themselves that they associate with their jobs and accomplishments. These ideas have nothing to do with reality, whether they are positive or negative.

Mirror gazing is a good way to really look at yourself. The eyes are said to be the windows to the soul, and you might find looking directly into your own eyes to be very uncomfortable. Try gazing at your own eyes for a few minutes every morning. You can also do this with a partner to increase love for each other. Remember, the main reason that you do not love yourself is that you cannot really see yourself due to a lack of perception. Any kind of modality that clears your mind and your perceptual lens assist you in self-love and compassion of others.

Compassion is itself not really a 'path' or means to self-love. What happens is that when you becoming more self-loving, you become more compassionate towards others. In terms of the shadow, what you see in others you detest, as it is alive within you. But when the shadow has been integrated, you are more compassionate to those who suffer from the issues that you have integrated. You recognize them more clearly because you used to have them, and your compassion is far greater because of the integration.

Discipline and focus can be a means to self-love. This entails moving away from automatic behaviors which are not serving you. But it can be very tricky to get the balance right between being dogmatic and disciplined. Some people can become extremists and are unable to enjoy the simple joys. Yet for the vast majority, the difficulty lies in a lack of discipline and constant indulgences.

In any case, advertising, social media, processed foods, alcohol, and cigarettes should be minimized as much as possible. If you really love your body, you will make the effort and treat it right with exercise and a reasonable diet.

Nothing really beats meditating on love and generating it as raw emotion. This is a professional practice for people who want to really attain a mastery of love. It is the most direct approach of really feeling the energy of love and directing it at an object and towards yourself.

Organization and Cleanliness

While this is secondary, try to clean up the outside environment as much as possible. This means that your room and desk is as clean as possible. You might also want to throw out some of your old stuff or do a garage sale. This is very therapeutic and should serve to clean the mind. You need to put yourself in a safe, clean, and organized environment.

You also want to rid yourself of any toxic relationships that you have. Toxic relationships in the home or workplace will sap your energy like nothing else. While you are angry, fearful, or ashamed, you are blocking the energy of love. Understand that it is not possible to feel a positive and negative emotion at the same time. So if you are fearful, you are not loving. However, this has an added benefit. If you can manage to generate loving emotions in the midst of a depression of crisis, then it is possible to drag yourself up. This takes a long time to master, and you need to practice being a loving person.

In any case, it is best to rid yourself of toxic relationships and to establish a community of people who are loving, compassionate, and kind. Keep all aspects of your inner and outer environment as clean as you can and be organized in all of your endeavors.

Chapter 5

The Complexity and Psychology of Self-Esteem

Assessing self-esteem can be quite problematic. The issue lies in the fact that self-esteem can fluctuate on a moment to moment basis throughout the day. It is also often related to a role or function. Some people can have millions of dollars while also battling social anxiety or depression. Others are excellent at dating but awful at work. However, it is significant that the confidence lies in the person's perception of himself or herself in that particular field.

Self-esteem stems from our attachment to something. For example, a chef might take pride in his status as a wonderful cook. And if you were disappointed in the food, the chef would be very unhappy compared to somebody who does not cook for a living. The same applies to any person who is proud of the role that he or she is doing.

And this is why self-love is on another level. It is not attached to anything. Because whenever you are attached to something out of identification, your validation stems from what others think.

Even if it is positive, it is still temporary. But self-love is non- dualistic and constant once you practice it.

Building Self-Esteem

There is no set routine for building self-esteem. While scientific studies have confirmed the benefits, they have been unable to provide a standardized means of improving self-esteem. This is because each human being is very complex and multifaceted.

Science understands almost nothing about how the human being perceives his or her reality and associates with the past and the present. And it has not made any inroads whatsoever into the dream sleep and its significance.

Many of the products and services designed to enhance self- esteem have the opposite effect of their stated purpose. People actually feel worse after taking them. This is because these products are services tend to be externally orientated, such as cosmetics, voice tonality, fancy clothes, and other superficial modalities. Even immersion can be difficult for those suffering from social anxiety and other issues. If a person is nervous speaking in front of a crowd, then forcing them to repeat this action could simply lead to a breakdown and further trauma.

On the flip side, there are definitely things that you can do. While there is no "one size fits all" approach that can help with self- esteem, every individual will respond well to certain healing modalities. The trick lies in finding out what this is and helping the individual to overcome it. This is what psychology and shadow work is all about. The person is able to see the difficulties more clearly using dream work, journaling, direct communication, hypnosis, and other forms of therapy. Once these demons are brought to the light of consciousness, they can dissipate.

Unfortunately, it is a lot harder than it sounds and these ingrained tendencies do not simply dissipate in the majority of instances.

Figuring out Self-Esteem

There is a constant debate within the spiritual and psychological community with regard to the 'correct' way forward with self-esteem and with healing in general. Some push for positivity, others shadow work. Some advocate integration, others say that 'letting go' is the best approach. Some state that balance and harmony are the ultimate pinnacles of healing, more dictate that creative chaos is the natural state of a universe that is constantly changing.

The fact is that all of these approaches will work at certain times for certain people. Some people might need to integrate the various parts of themselves, while other patients might really need to let go of issues. As always, the best way to build confidence in a patient suffering from depression or low self-esteem of some sort is to let them communicate their feelings openly first and establish an open dialogue. Instead of simply pushing therapy on the person, alternative therapies could be suggested. In the way, the person uses his or her own power and resources to come up with creative answers. And it could be anything from painting to diet to meditation to going back to university.

Practical Ways to Build Self-Esteem

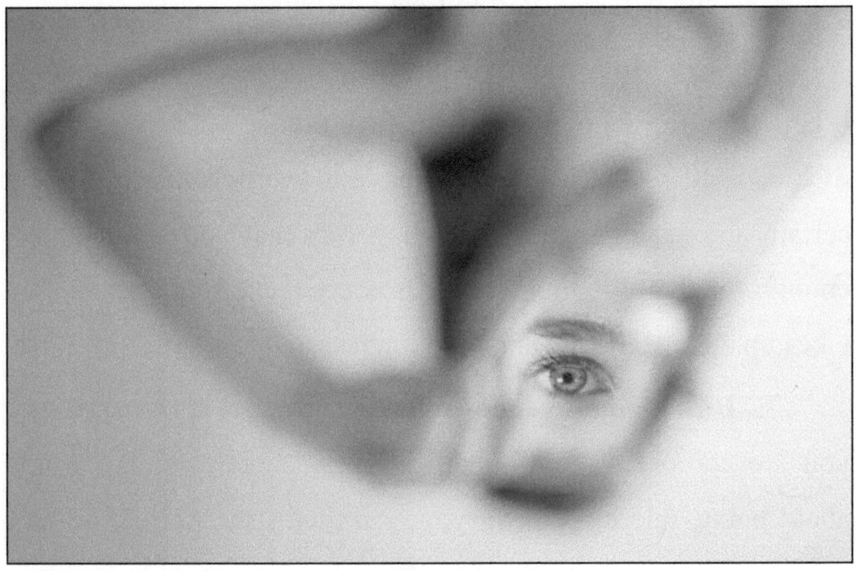

As complex and multifaceted as building self-esteem might be, there are still a number of down to earth and practical ways to enhance it. Taking yourself out of situations where you are not confident is equally as important as putting yourself in places where you have high levels of self-esteem. The following are 7 practical ways to build self-esteem.

1. **Put Your Health First** - Always put your health and well-being first. Nothing is more important than being stress-free in a healthy body. This will also involve a certain amount of

discipline. Exercise regularly and tend to diet, as health is attractive and will lead to self-esteem. By looking and feeling better, people will also start to treat you better.

2. **Save Money** - Regardless of your beliefs about money, it is needed to function. And you should have a healthy amount of it at hand so that you do not have to worry about it. Save a certain amount of money and budget so that you always have enough for the bills in advance. Anxiety and stress over money takes up a lot of mental and emotional resources.

3. **Build Competence** - Whatever your role is, make sure you are competent at it. Like a lack of money, if you worry about being able to perform your job then your well-being will suffer. Competence is one of the best things to assist in building confidence. Whatever you are good at, try to get better.

4. **Focus** - Do not exert all of your resources trying to do too many things at once. Keep it simple and focus on doing one thing at a time. Many people overexert themselves with too many tasks or go the other way with too much vacation time. You can use focus to build money and competence slowly over time.

5. **Meditation** - Health, money, and competence are the building blocks of a healthy human being. But after this, it is

time to take it to the next level and build confidence that is hard to shake in any circumstances. Meditation can assist in detaching you from reality so you are not as affected by the thoughts and opinions of others any more. It won't work overnight, but it definitely works.

6. **Inner Assessment** - You need to identify core fears and beliefs that you have and find some way to work on them. There are online questionnaires which can help you to identify what your beliefs are. You can use affirmations to help change these beliefs or work on them using physical activities.

7. **Reframe** - Reframing is a great way to put yourself into a good mood. When something happens that you do not like, simply list the good that came out of it. Everything can be reframed, and everything is subjective in any case. Nobody sees the same situation in the same way.

Chapter 6

Mastering Thoughts and Emotions

It is not disputed within esoteric circles that the quality of your thoughts will determine the nature of your reality. And thought is really just a habit. If you can really change your thoughts you will be able to control what you experience. Even if you end up in a negative environment, you can still control your reaction to it.

Moreover, a negative environment is most likely only negative because you have some kind of negative belief surrounding it, which you can change.

Mastering Thoughts

Thoughts gather momentum and tend to perpetuate themselves. And so, the rich get richer and the poor get poorer on this planet not due to any kind of structured inequality, but simply due to thoughts of poverty perpetuating themselves and thoughts of riches perpetuating themselves. People prefer to adopt a victim mindset than to take control of their thoughts and focus continually on wealth and solutions. It is so much easier to blame a villain than to accept responsibility. It is also far lazier and accomplishes nothing at all.

The primary reason that people have not mastered their thoughts is not a lack of information. It is a lack of dedication and consistency. People have a habit of instantly reacting to negative news and events without understanding the power of their own minds. They are the ones generating the stress, anxiety and worry as a result of their own powers of observation.

Gaining power over your thoughts is a lifelong endeavor. But it is the only real task that you have to do, as it determines everything.

Mastering Emotions

Thoughts and emotions are interlinked. While thoughts lead to emotions, it is entirely possible to learn to leverage emotions without any thoughts whatsoever. This is even more powerful. It is not the thought that generates the power, but the emotional energy behind it. So you can go directly to the source. Of course, the most powerful emotion is love, and you should try to master this if possible. Love can be generated if you place your thoughts on people that you adore. Over time, you will be able to summon the energy directly. This will not happen overnight but it will greatly increase your power and charisma.

Some events can generate an immensely negative reaction from a person due to previous trauma. And this can be very difficult to deal with. But the principles remain the same, though the intensity might be far worse. You have to find a way to deactivate the negative energy and focus on positive energy.

This does not mean that you are ignoring the problem. A problem would imply that there is something wrong with you that needs to be fixed. But reality is perception, and you need to change your mental and emotional lens to see things from the perspective of the higher self - who you really are:

"We do not see things as they are, we see them as we are" (The Talmud)

A Note on Beliefs

Beliefs deserve to be examined. They are often mentioned but rarely explored in detail. A belief is simply a thought that has been repeated over and over again. It becomes ingrained in the human being as a fact, though this is not really the case. As such, these beliefs can easily be deactivated by people who turn their attention toward positive thoughts. The new beliefs replace the old.

Again, it is not possible to feel both love and hate at the same time. They are opposites. But if you have a belief about someone that results in the energy of hatred, then you will continue to have this belief unless the thought chain is interrupted. Activating the exact opposite is key to deactivating a negative belief. However, you need to use meditation as an intermediary. If you are in anger or despair, first you need to meditate and slow down. Then you need to access the opposite belief.

Deep beliefs are often the biggest obstacle to new states of awareness. For example, you might have read all of the material but deep down do not feel you are worthy of a partner. There are a wide number of erroneous beliefs such as “resources are scarce and we must compete” and “you have to work hard to get rich”. These beliefs are completely inaccurate. Everybody has their own set of beliefs which need to be scrutinized. It is not possible to evolve with limiting beliefs. But you can use the power of habits to remove them over time.

Chapter 7

The Power of Habits

The power of habits is not to be underestimated. A mature understanding of habits and how to use them is fundamental to becoming a fully whole and integrated human being. Because your habits are the primary determinant of who you are and who you become:

"Repetition of the same thought or action develops into a habit, which, repeated frequently enough, becomes an automatic reflex" (Vincent Norman Peel)

What you do every day will change who you are. The issue is that most people have poor habits which they complete every day without thinking about them. Your habits will help you to correct some of your subconscious tendencies.

The Subconscious

Consider that half of all of your daily activities are automatic. You do not put any conscious awareness into them. Habits are a way for our brains to conserve energy over time, and they are vital to our functioning. Imagine if you had to calculate every step to work beforehand, how to make your breakfast, open the front door, take each step to the car, start the ignition, drive in busy traffic etc.

Thankfully, our subconscious takes care of all of it. The brain is only capable of remembering between 5-9 facts at a time. The rest is passed to the subconscious for processing. When you do something once, you can complete it the next time around on autopilot far more easily. Most of your habits are driven by unconscious fears that you are not yet aware of. Correcting habits can have the effect of correcting these fears, though it takes time.

How to Master Habits

Everything that you do is no more than a habit. Some habits are incredibly deeply ingrained. The longer that a habit is put in place, the harder it is to replace. Think of the example of a person who has been smoking for 30 years, constantly used to taking smoking breaks with friends and smoking at home. But it is just as easy to make a habit out of going to the gym or meditating than it is to smoke or drink alcohol. As everybody knows it is not the gym or meditation that is difficult. It is the thought of the gym or meditation and getting to the place itself.

It takes 3 days for the body to get used to a different kind of diet. In drug rehabilitation, the first 3 days are the most difficult, and after this, the patient will have a much easier time staying away. This is because the body is physically dependent on the drug and has adapted to its presence. After 3 days, it will have adapted to functioning without the drug. However, this is only the physical side of things.

Scientific studies have established that it takes 3 weeks for a habit to become ingrained. After 3 weeks, it is likely that the person will continue doing it afterwards. So if you really want to master a habit, the 3 day and 21-day marks are the most important. After these points, it will become a lot easier. Once a habit has been installed, it just becomes second nature. It does not really matter what it is. This is the beauty of habits once you understand them and use them to your benefit.

Of course, the ultimate habit that you want to maintain is positive thoughts. The minute you find yourself thinking of a negative thought, try to change it to something positive.

Overtime, even this will become second nature, and negative thoughts will have become a thing of the past. This is the ultimate habit to adopt, so it is best to start with other practices such as meditation or diet first.

Good Habits To Master

Affirmations are one of the best ways to enhance self-esteem, as long as they are done correctly. However, it should be borne in mind that the affirmations need to be believable. If the affirmation is too far from where you are, then it won't be believed and will just remind you of what you are not. The affirmation also needs to be in the present tense and not a negation. "I am not poor" is reinforcing poverty, while "I am rich" reinforces riches.

There are an infinite amount of habits to take on board, so you will need to be selective. The best habits will depend on the person in question. It could be meditating, drinking a smoothie, visualizing your perfect day, or just making your bed before work. Also, consider turning off your WiFi at night and reducing technology usage before sleep.

The time just prior to sleeping and just upon waking is one where you have access to the theta state while still conscious. If you can try to manifest a positive emotion in these states, your day and night will run much more smoothly. Lucid dreaming is another modality which can help you get what you want.

The morning is the best time to complete a task or engage in a positive habit. Studies have demonstrated that willpower is highest in the morning and tends to wane as the day goes on. So start your day off as well as you possibly can. The worst thing that you can do is roll out of bed, look at your emails, shower, grab a slice of toast, and head to work. When you are looking at your emails you are basically downloading stress first thing in the morning. The morning time is sacred and you need to keep some space there for relaxation. Sadly, most people are stressed about work and do not even give themselves the morning to relax.

Habits are Hard

Whatever kind of habit you adopt, remember to stick with it for at least 3 weeks. And do it first thing in the morning. Over time, it will become second nature to you. Incorporate your habits one at a time so you do not get overwhelmed. Habits are very difficult to break out of once they become ingrained. They are engrained so strongly in the brain that they can even survive brain damage. On the other hand, this can be a good thing if you adopt positive habits. As per Warren Buffett:

"The chains of habit are too light to be felt until they are too heavy to be broken"

As difficult as habits may be to break, if you stick with it, the benefits can be phenomenal. You can find yourself on a never-ending spiral of self-development. One habit after the next can be broken, from the smallest to the biggest. But people often need to identify one keystone habit that will result in a change in all the others. You can use the power of habit to find your true self and establish unshakable self-esteem.

Chapter 8

Creative Ways to Boost Self- Love

Meditation, organization, discipline, purification, diet and more have huge benefits. But they can be very stale and lifeless for many people, despite their necessity. You do not have to stick to these aesthetic practices. In fact, loving yourself is anything but boring. It should be the most enjoyable journey of a lifetime.

Because you are literally doing things that make you happy at intensity.

Creativity and Imagination

Creativity is a means of accessing parts of you that have lain dormant due to societal conventions. As stated in the beginning, we shut down our creative, spiritual, emotional and physical centers due to the pressure to conform. The challenge lies in opening up these faculties at a later stage.

The hallmarks of self-love are authenticity and originality. Creativity can only come from inside of you. But most of our society consists of copy cats. People copy each other all the time. Think of the number of online eBooks on "how to make money online". The same old advice repeated and sold over and over and over. It is not possible to make money online by simply taking another person's formula and repeating it. You need to be original to be truly successful. This is why you should stay away from prescripted formulas for success. Even if they genuinely worked for the original creator, they will not work for you *because they are not your creation.* This is an important point.

Creative Practices

One of the biggest and most powerful ways to boost self-love is to go on a wild trip. Do something that you have never done before. Better yet, do something that is far outside of your comfort zone, like quit your job and travel the world. It is guaranteed to open up previously inaccessible avenues of thought and emotion that you never knew you had.

There could be little more disappointing than travelling down the same road with a few variations along the line within the same corporation. Wages increases and another title are immensely boring to people who are living their true lives. They are typically no more than abstractions that people use to content themselves with very unsatisfying lives.

There are a variety of ways to improve the imagination. Bear in mind that it is an ongoing and never-ending process, but one that gets more satisfying as times goes by. The best practices include:

- Creative writing.
- Art.
- Martial arts.
- Dancing.
- Singing.
- Cooking.
- Travel.
- Anything else that you love to do.

Obviously, the list is not exhaustive. And there is room for creativity in logical subjects such as accounting or math. But it has to be applied dynamically and used often by the person.

Otherwise, the imagination will lie dormant as the person continues to rely on textbooks and manuals written by somebody else. The way to enhance creativity lies in persistence. If you are painting, then you need to try and paint a painting every single day. You will have certain insights and eureka moments now and again, but you cannot tell when they are going to happen.

Regardless of what creative activity you are doing, you need to engage in it every day. Creativity can also help to unroot subconscious tendencies. For example, characters in a story or images in a painting are reflected in the inner psyche. While you may not be able to discuss such things in public, they can be expressed through creative means.

The Intuition

The intuition is an incredibly underappreciated aspect of every individual. It holds the answer to every question and needs to be relied upon. The intuitive faculties have to be developed over time. They largely evolve when a person detaches from the rational processes associated with strenuous mental thought.

However, the mind is very limited and can only process a small amount of information.

Intuition, creativity, and imagination are very tightly linked. The processes that you can use to increase creativity are the same ones that you can use to increase your intuitive power. Intuition is your biggest friend when it comes to making life choices. There are thousands of ways to increase self-love, but only a few will be perfect for you at a specific time.

And it is a lot easier than people make it out. If there is anything that really stands out and that you think would work, go for it.

Don't dismiss your desires and goals as irrelevant. They are the single greatest signposts that you have. Above all, find something that you love to do and be creative in doing it. This is your true self and this is empowering. If you love yourself, give yourself the gift of doing what you love 24/7 without caring what other people think of you. It is the pinnacle of human achievement to be uniquely you without input from anyone else.

CONCLUSION

Finding out who you really are and generating self-love for yourself is the most rewarding experience that you can have. The spiritual term is self-realization and is beyond the understanding of those who have not experienced it.

Yet some are closer than others and will exhibit higher levels of self-esteem. After all, confidence is simply being more aligned with who you really are. The people who try to be something they are not are the ones who are underconfident. It takes a remarkable amount of resources to put up a facade and it is immensely energizing when you align yourself with your own divinity. In the words of the Greeks:

"Know thy self and you shalt know the Gods and all the universe"

Printed by Libri Plureos GmbH in Hamburg,
Germany